Angel S Reference Book

written by

Debbie Brewer

Artwork by

Nikki Zalewski

Copyright © 2019 Debbie Brewer

First published in May 2019 by Lulu.com

Distributed by Lulu.com

All rights reserved. No part of this book may be reproduced by any mechanical, photographic, or electronic process, or in the form of a phonographic recording. Nor may it be stored in a retrieval system, transmitted or otherwise be copied for public or private use, other than for fair use as brief quotations embodied in articles and reviews, without prior written permission of the author.

ISBN-13: 978-0-244-18840-5

First Edition

The author of this book does not dispense medical advice or prescribe the use of any technique as a form of treatment for physical, emotional or medical problems. The intent of the author is only to offer information of a general nature to help you in your search for emotional and spiritual well-being. In the event you use any of the information in this book for yourself, the author assumes no responsibility for your actions.

Contents

Foreword

Coincidences

Sychronicities

Signs

Finally

Summary of Signs

Also By Debbie Brewer

Connect With The Author

Foreword

Firstly, I thank the angels who have drawn your attention to this little book.

It is written with the intention to provide a quick and simple reference guide, listing and detailing all the ways that the heavenly angels may choose to communicate with you.

Use this guide to know and recognise when you have received an angelic sign, showing you the presence of a divine angel near you, helping, supporting, reassuring, comforting, guiding, shielding and protecting you.

Angels will always be ready and willing to answer your requests through their radiance, grace and love of mankind, to change your life for the better.

Coincidences

Do we have full understanding or control over every single event in our lives?

Sometimes things happen for which we have no rational explanation. They could be random. But sometimes it can be surprisingly well timed. And there are times when something very simple will occur, that you will notice, to which there is no earthly human logical reasoning. This is when an angel is communicating with you, through coincidences, synchronicities and signs.

Coincidences

Coincidences occur when two events, which have nothing presently to do which each other, happen within a very short space of time, and then a link between them becomes apparent retrospectively.

When you ask for help from an angel, or even acknowledge your faith in angels, coincidences start to happen. The more you look for them, the more you recognise them happening.

Coincidence is God's way of remaining anonymous

- *Albert Einstein*

There are three types of coincidences:

- Sign Coincidences
- Right Time Coincidence
- Right place Coincidences

Sign Coincidences

Some coincidences are signs that occur soon after a request for help from an angel has been made.

For example, you may have asked for help to heal a sick child, and then very soon after, you see a feather float down in front of you, from no apparent source, or a light brush against your arm, when there is no-one there. This is a coincidence. It is a communication from an angel to show they have heard your request and they are sharing with you their intention to help you.

Right Time Coincidences

Other coincidences are called right time coincidences. These are where several related situations happen within a short space of time.

For example, you may have asked an angel for guidance on coping with a broken relationship. Very soon a song plays on the radio that capsulises how you are feeling. Or the phone rings and it is an old friend ringing for a chat. Or someone new unexpectedly enters your life in a random way. These are communications and interventions from your angel, providing guidance and help.

Right Place Coincidences

Another form of coincidences are right place coincidences. These occur when you just happen to be in the right place for a situation that you have asked for to be played out.

For example, you may have asked an angel for help to find a job as a receptionist. Very soon, you go to a friend's BBQ and happen to meet with a friend whose brother is looking for a receptionist for his company. Or, you are having your hair cut at your regular hairdressers and the receptionist there tells you she is leaving and they need to fill her position. Or you might be having a coffee in a café, and there is a newspaper left on your table. The first page you turn to has an advert for your perfect job. This is angelic intervention, clearing the way and helping you to follow the path you have chosen. Your angel has ensured everything is in place to guide you.

Synchronicities

Synchronicity involves synchronous timing. It is when two separate events occur at the same time, which have meanings emerge when viewed together.

The sum of the whole is greater than the sum of the parts

-The Theory of Synergy

When one thing happens, it can be considered as chance. But when two or more things happen at the same time, that is angelic intervention and communication.

For example, you may have asked an angel to reassure that you are following the right path for your life. Very soon, your favourite song plays on the radio. At the same time, a rainbow appears in the sky, it stops raining, the sun comes out and a small child randomly waves at you. These events are synchronised by your angel to provide you with the reassurance you requested. You will know. You will find yourself smiling inside and overcome by a feeling of calm.

Signs

Signs can occur within coincidences or synchronous events, but they can also occur on their own. They can be one off events, created by angels to help, guide or protect you.

These signs may be direct and obvious or indirect and more subtle. But the more you look for them, the more you will get used to recognising them and the more often you will see them.

It might be something you see, feel or tangibly touch, and when you find yourself saying, "It's a sign", then your intuition is right. This is you accepting communication from an angel.

Some signs will be personal, and will only have meaning for you. But you will see and understand them if you look. They tell us the angels are near and they give us a message to interpret.

Some common signs are often used by angels to communicate their presence.

Feathers

If you see a feather in an unusual place, or it floats down to you unexpectedly, then an angel is letting you know of their presence. It may be any size, shape or colour, and it may be in response to your request for assistance, or simply to reassure or comfort you during a difficult time. A white feather will arrive at a time when you are most in need, to let you know you are not alone.

Rainbows

Rainbows have well known scientific explanations. But have you ever stared at a rainbow and still felt the magic? Maybe it's shape does not look quite right, or it has occurred without rain, or it has happened at a time soon after you have asked for a sign to reassure or reaffirm some situation in your life. It may be a double rainbow or a rainbow orb or halo around an object. The angels are using this phenomenon to guide you.

Bells

If you can hear a bell ring, even the slightest tinkle or chirp of a bell, and there is no apparent reason for a bell to ring, then an angel is near you.

Voices

You may think you have heard someone lightly call your name when there is no one around. Or you may hear a word, or several words. It may be that you hear a voice, but cannot understand the words that are being spoken. Ask the angel to speak clearer or louder, so you can hear and understand them. It is usually a quiet voice, often a whisper, a calm serene tone of assurance, that is letting you know of the caring presence of an angel.

Coins

A single coin in an unusual place signifies an angel is near. If it is on the pavement of a road you were thinking of walking down, then do so. If it is on the doorstep of a building, shop or home, then enter it. These are signs being left for you by an angel who wishes to guide you along your path.

Also, you may find when you look carefully at a coin that you have found or that someone has given you, that it may have an image or numbers that resonate with some profound meaning for you.

Changes in the Localised Climate

When angels are very present, the localised climate around you may alter. The temperature may get slightly warmer or cooler, but still remaining comfortable. The light may appear just a little brighter, or the room and its furnishings may ever so slightly glow, almost unnoticeably so. The air might feel only the slightest bit heavier and you might notice not much more than a tingle of a movement of the air around you.

If you were not open to the idea of angels, if you did not have faith, you would not even notice these changes, but by being spiritually aware, you will come to notice when the presence of angels affect the local environment surrounding you.

Media

If you have requested assistance from an angel, there is every possibility they could provide guidance by directing you to an answer to be found within media. You may come across a relevant thread in social media, or a helpful answer on the TV, without having been intentionally looking there for answers. It may be that you notice a message on a local bill board or a certain street name or shop sign. It will hold a meaning for you. The angels can use any avenue of communication to connect with you.

Clouds

Seeing specific shapes in clouds, such as hearts and other shapes, can be signs of guidance. You may even be able to see the shape of an angel or angel wings, a sure sign that they are there for you.

Lights and Orbs

Angels exude pure divine light. Orbs are said to be 'vehicles of angels'. These are opaque spherical features which usually present themselves in photos, but which can also be observed by the naked eye. Sometimes you may see a shower of light, a shimmer, sparkle, flash or an orb, of any colour, in the corner of your eye, but when you look directly at it, it's not there. You should believe in what you have noticed. It has caught your eye for a reason. It may be an unusual shimmer of light off an object, like an unfocused reflection of something that isn't there. This is the presence of an angel.

Feelings

Angels may communicate with us through our sixth sense, our psychic abilities. You may become aware of the presence of angels through clairvoyance, clairaudience, or any of the other spiritual abilities. Remember, you can work on improving these abilities and increase you spiritual awareness of angels.

You may simply 'feel' the presence of an angel. You may experience a subtle brush across your arm or neck. Or the placement of a hand on your back or shoulder. You may sense the presence of someone with you when you are in an empty room. You may feel emotionally and inexplicably loved. This is when an angel has wrapped you in the comfort of their wings, surrounding you with the protection and comfort of their purest love. Trust this feeling. It is real. It doesn't lie to you. It is truth.

Wing Symbols

Images of angelic wings are signs of angels, such as wings drawn in dust, or sand, or in the condensation on a window pane.

Music

Rarely, you may find yourself hearing angelic music or singing from no apparent source. This is angelic communication.

Also, angels might use music to guide you or comfort you. You might find yourself listening to a piece of music that can change your mood, or provide a specific meaning to you. Or you may notice a recurring piece of music playing, or several pieces of music with similar themes. It could be that a particular piece of music invokes an old memory of a place or a person and this maybe a sign that you should re-visit this place or contact that person. Sometimes a song may just start playing in your mind. Embrace this. This is angelic intervention on your behalf, for your benefit.

Clock Chimes

Sometimes you may notice a clock chime, or part chime, or even just give a slight ping, when it is not supposed to. When this happens, an angel is near you.

Scent

You may suddenly smell a fragrance or scent, that has no apparent origin. This is a sign of an angel near you. It may be flowery, it will always be pleasant, and it might invoke a memory. If it does, then the angel near you has deliberately wanted you to remember something for a reason. You may even find you have a recurrent unexplained fragrance that you may come to recognise as that of a specific angel, maybe your guardian angel.

Babies, Young Children and Pets

You may notice that sometimes babies and young children will suddenly look in a particular direction and laugh or clap or even seem to be communicating with something that to us, as adults, is not there. Similarly, your pet might notice something, or bark at something when there is seemingly nothing there. They are responding to the presence of angels. Their pure untainted innocence and unquestioning love allows them to be able to connect at a higher spiritual level.

Objects Falling

Sometimes, an object may fall out in front of you. It may be a book falling off a shelf. Or a ring falls from the table. Maybe a coin drops from your purse. In every case, carefully regard the item. What is the title of the book? Did it fall open on a particular page? What is the significance of the ring? What does it bring to mind? What does the image, wording or numbers on the coin mean to you? Whatever it is that has fallen before you, it will hold a meaning that you will be able to identify with. It is the guiding intervention of an angel, leading you to an answer or solution to something on your mind.

Dreams

When an angel visits you in a dream, listen to them. They may be giving you a message. Or maybe they want to lead you somewhere in your dream. Go with them. They are with you and they are trying to offer you some kind of guidance, maybe to answer a question you have asked or to help you find the correct path to take, or to protect you.

Repetition

Angels can use repetition of an event to draw your attention. For example, if you hear the same name repeated by three unrelated people within a matter of days, then this may be a sign from the angels that you should get in touch with that person. Hence the phrase, *pay attention when things happen in threes.* (White, L, nd).

Identical Numbers

A sequence of three or more identical numbers shown to you unexpectedly is a way for angels to get you to stop and pay attention. They are trying to tell you something. You need to ponder what is on your mind at that time. Pay attention to it. The answer is within you. The angels are using the identical sequence to guide you.

Unique Numbers

As an individual, you will also have a unique number that angels will use to connect with you, to make you aware of something. You may not know your unique number, but the angels will have presented it to you in the past, and they will do again. It is for you to notice and become aware of. It will be a random three digit number that keeps popping up unexpectedly in your life.

There will be other numbers, of not necessarily just three digits, that will only hold a relevance to you personally when you see them because you can refer them to something specific in your life. For example, maybe you keep seeing the numbers of the house where you grew up, or the numbers within your date of birth. Again, the angels are letting you know of their presence. They are offering you guidance and support.

Number Manipulation

Another typical angelic communication can come from a relevance emerging from a manipulation of numbers, such as the 216th number of the Fibonacci sequence.

In the lowest choir of regular angels there are legions upon legions upon legions of angels. A legion is said to be up to 6000 angels, based on the Roman definition of a legion. Therefore, there are 6000 x 6000 x 6000 angels, in this choir, which totals 216,000,000,000 angels. In sacred geometry, there is a geometric number sequence called the Fibonacci Numbers, first recognised by Pingala, circa 250 BC. The 216th number in the Fibonacci sequence is 61922045166659013522867538786329787426939612 and if you add up all these individual numbers, they add up to 216. An interesting coincidence in itself. But there's more: This specific number is significant in many cultures, and it is believed the hidden name of God contains 216 characters. This is also an example of another numerical coincidence; an angelic connection to the total number of regular angels in the last choir.

Another example of number manipulation is when all numbers in a sequence are eventually added to result in one number. For example, the number 854 has the same meaning as the number 8, because 8 + 5 + 4 = 17 and then 1 + 7 = 8.

Number Patterns

To one person, a pattern of numbers may mean nothing, but to another person, a certain pattern may make them take note and pay attention. They may not know why, but with time and thought, the meaning will become apparent. For example, it may be a run of numbers that are all even or all odd. Or it may be a pattern such as 1,3,5,7... or any pattern that you recognise.

In fact, anything that appears to be a pattern to you, that makes you sit up and take note, is an angelic intervention, an invite from an angel letting you know that they are there, ready to help, guide and support you. It may not necessarily even be numeric, it may be any form of pattern, presenting itself from any corner of your material life, be they alphabetic, colour, sound, visual etc. Be spiritually aware. Take time to listen and notice. Before long, you will be seeing many patterns around you and you will be feeling the strong presence of loving angels supporting and guiding along the true path of your life. And it will be an immensely powerful and uplifting awakening experience.

Finally

As your faith grows and your spiritual awareness strengthens, you will learn to look for signs and be open to receiving them. Connection and communication with angels will become easier and more commonplace. They will find ways to guide you, protect you, and assist you in your requests for help, always leading you on your correct path, helping you find the true value and meaning of your life.

Yet you still have freewill. You are not forced to follow the guidance of angels. They cannot control you and they cannot stop you from taking an opposing path to the one they suggest. It is your choice. But know, that the angels will always be working for you, never against you and they will always do their best for you.

Always pay attention. Always be open and ready to recognise and acknowledge a sign and the presence of an angel. And always express your gratitude for their time, interest and divine love for you.

Summary of Signs

Sign Coincidences

Right Time Coincidences

Right Place Coincidences

Synchronicities

Feathers

Rainbows

Bells

Voices

Coins

Changes in the Localised Climate

Media

Clouds

Lights and Orbs

Feelings

Wing Symbols

Music

Clock Chimes

Scent

Babies, Young Children and Pets

Objects Falling

Dreams

Repetition

Identical Numbers

Unique Numbers

Number Manipulation

Number Patterns

Also by Debbie Brewer

If you liked this book, then you may also like

Understand Angels, Their Mission, Guidance and Connection with You

Angels are always ready and willing to help you. Learn how to communicate with the angelic

realm and understand the immense wisdom of angels for help, support, healing, guidance and protection. Embrace your spiritual awareness to let the eternal powerful love of the angels guide you along your true life's path towards light and enlightenment and change your life for the better. Get to know these wonderful heavenly beings, your Guardian Angel, the Archangels and which angels to connect with. Recognise the signs and acknowledge the presence of divine angels in your life. Angels are waiting for you to discover the beauty and magnificence of angelic connection with them. Their grace, splendour and love is radiant to all who search it.

And

Archangels, A Pocket reference Book

This is an ideal simple little go to reference book, listing and detailing the powerful Archangels who are always ready to answer your requests, using their immense wisdom and love for mankind to provide help, support, healing, guidance and protection. Use this guide to choose which divine Archangel you wish to communicate with, who would be most beneficial for your specific requests and through their radiance and graceful help, change your life for the better.

And

Sacred Geometry Book of History, Meanings and How To Create Them

Why is it that we are so drawn to and enticed by sacred geometry? They start with simple mathematical shapes, that combine to create elaborate illustrations of such beauty and

elegance that we marvel at them. Beliefs, religious, spiritual and cultural, have been historically attached to them. The specific design and creation of each individual sacred geometric pattern is thought, among many cultures, not only to demonstrate an understanding of specific universal concepts, but to hold powers of mystical possibilities. The aim of this book is to provide an understanding of the history, creation and meanings of sacred geometry for those who are new to the subject, and to open an insight into the beliefs placed upon them with the hope that it will inspire the reader's interest and imagination and increase their enthusiasm. Enjoy learning how such simple shapes can evolve into inspiring and powerful patterns that weave through the fabric of our entire universe and reality.

Connect with the author

www.debbiebrewer.co.uk

https://www.facebook.com/DebbieBrewerPoetry

www.instagram.com/poetrytreasures

www.twitter.com/poetrytreasure

Printed in Great Britain
by Amazon